AF394705

Count the Phonemes

Written by
Stephen Rickard

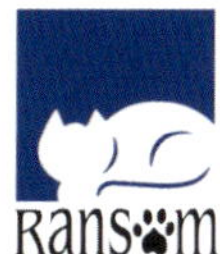
Ransom

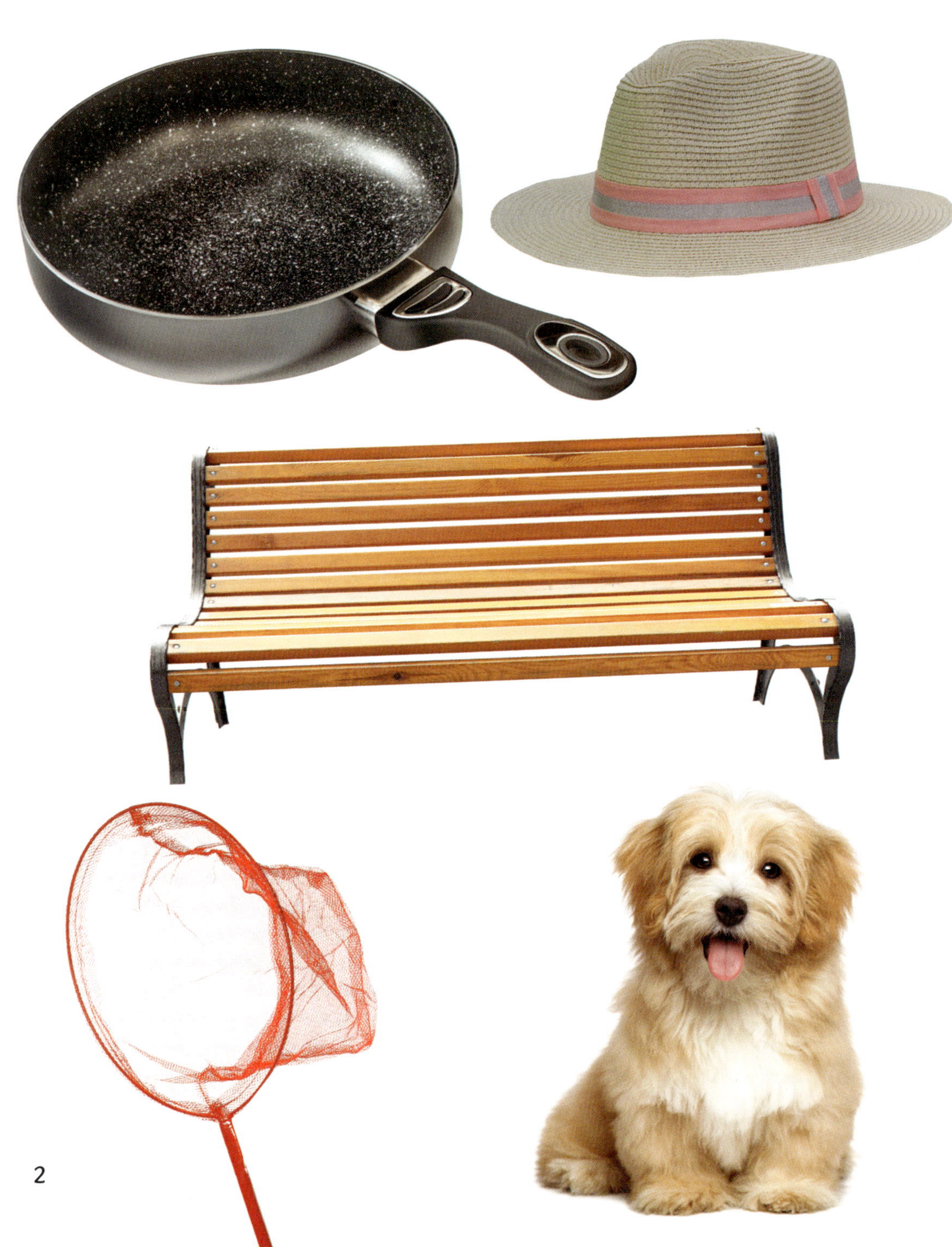

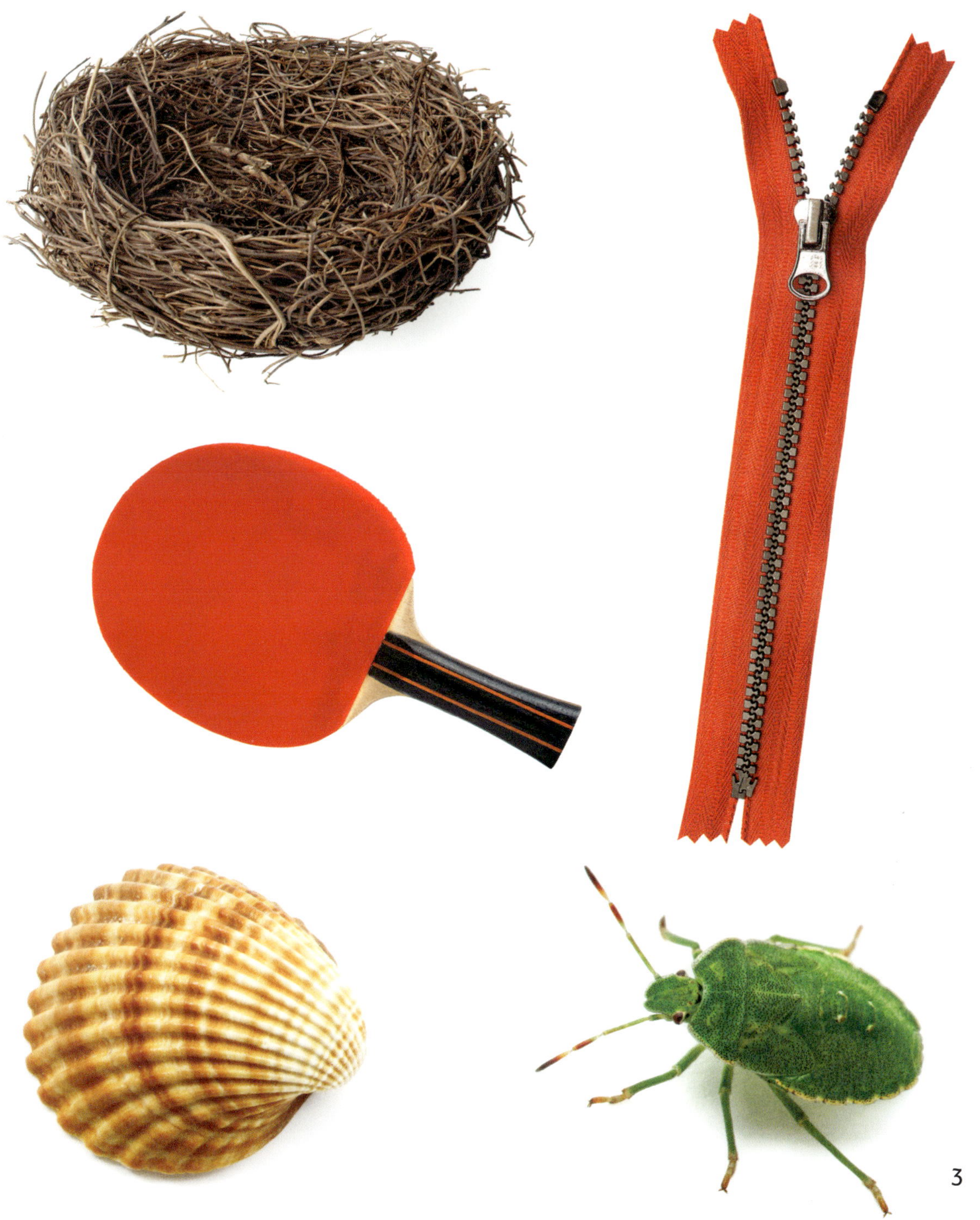

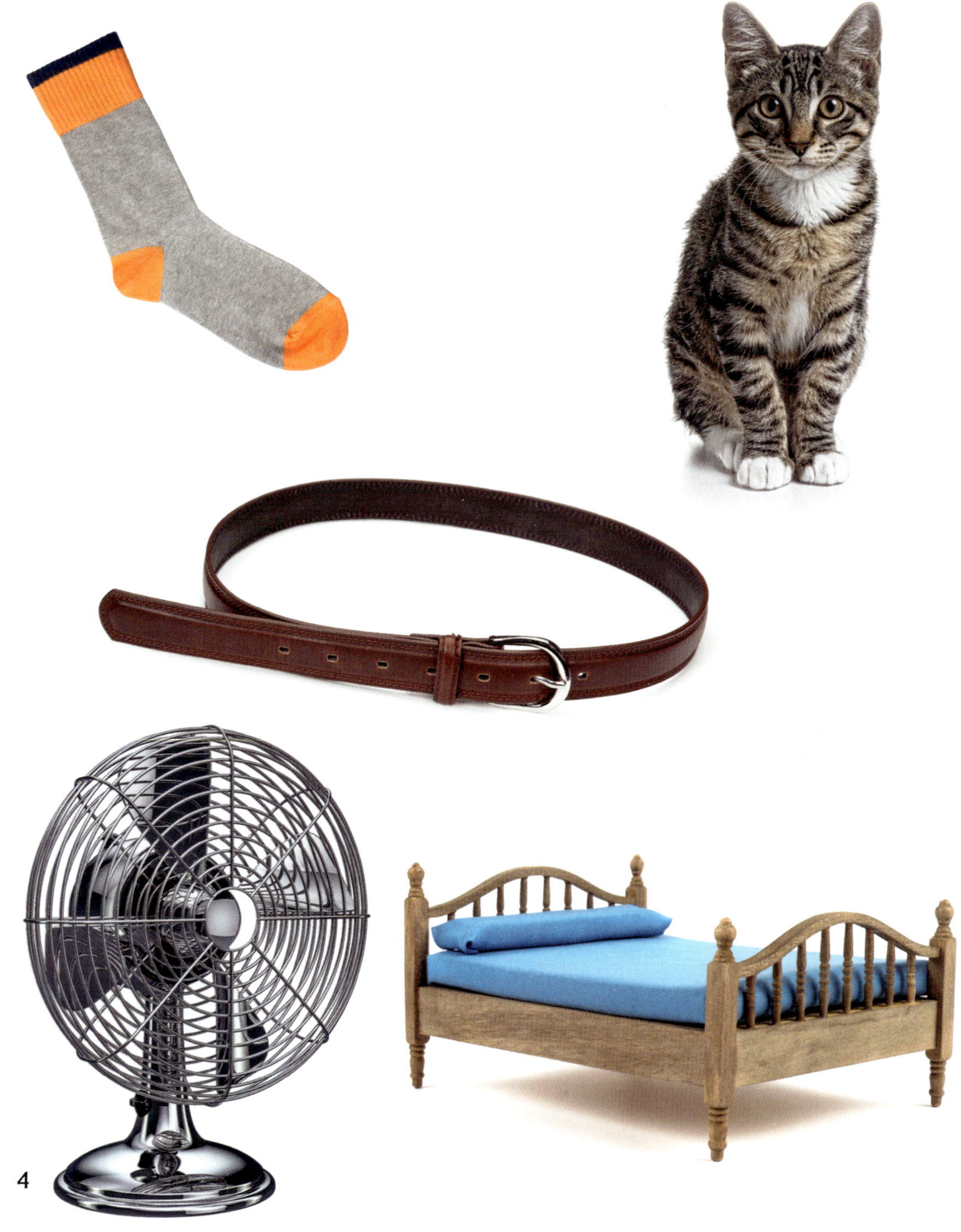

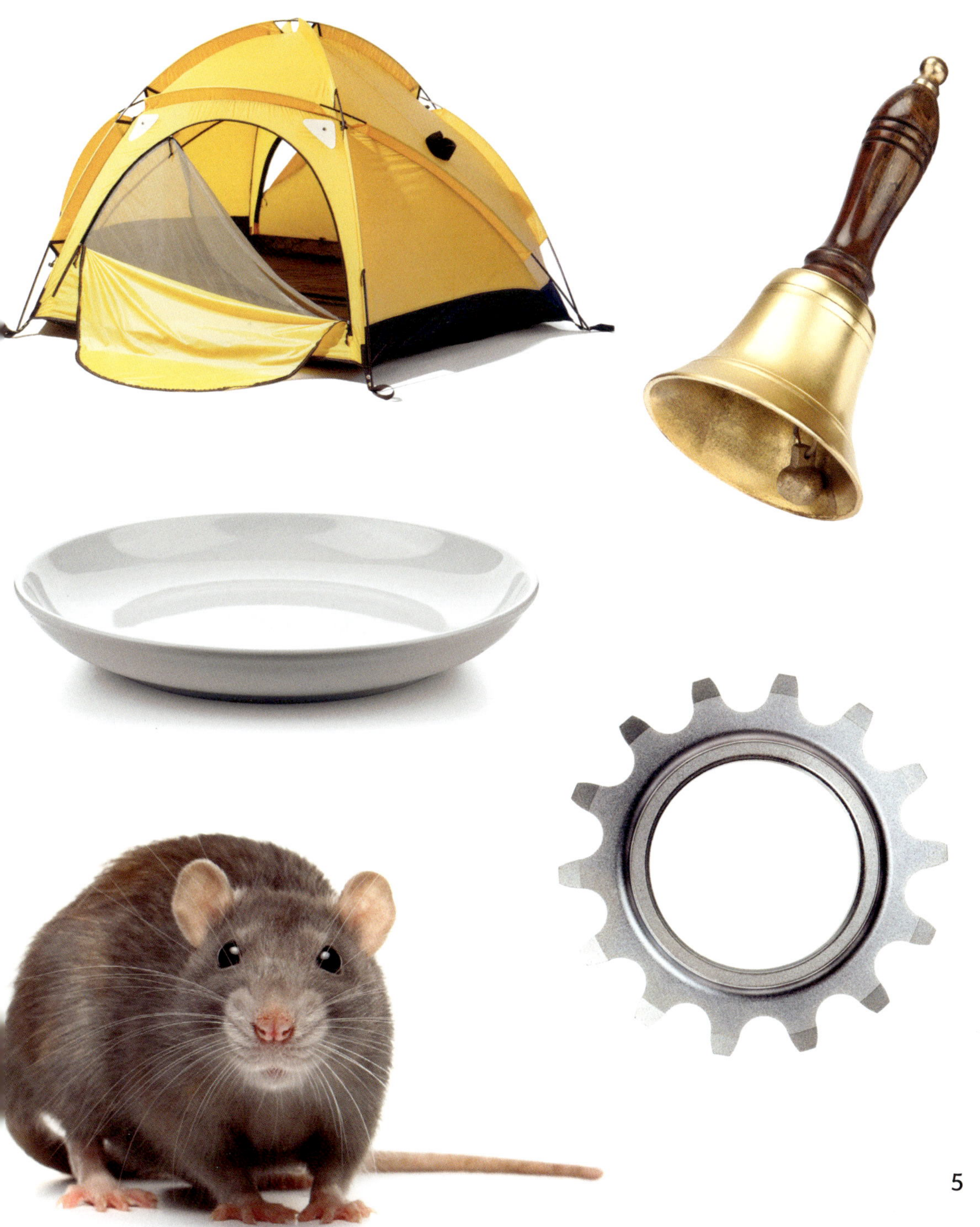

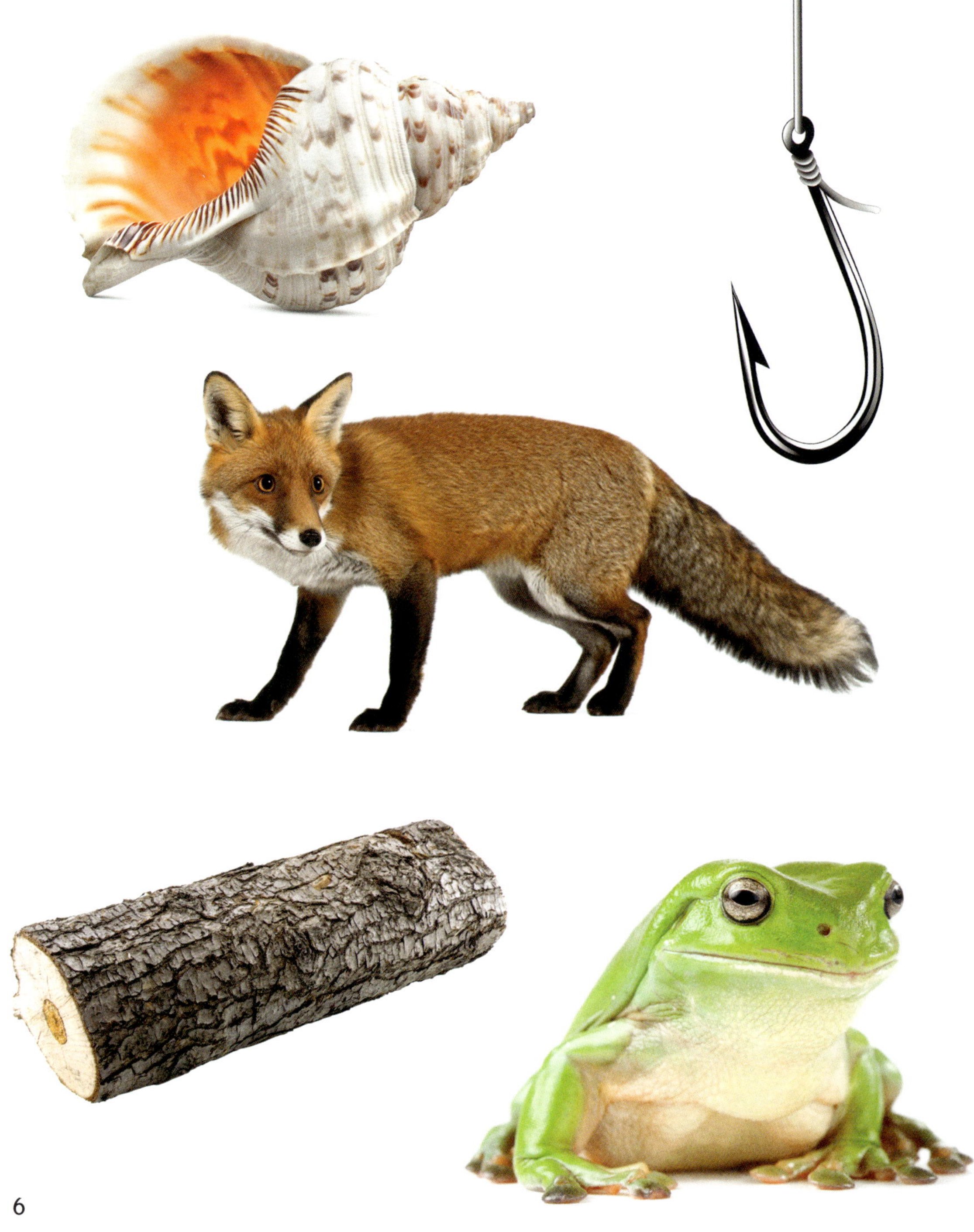

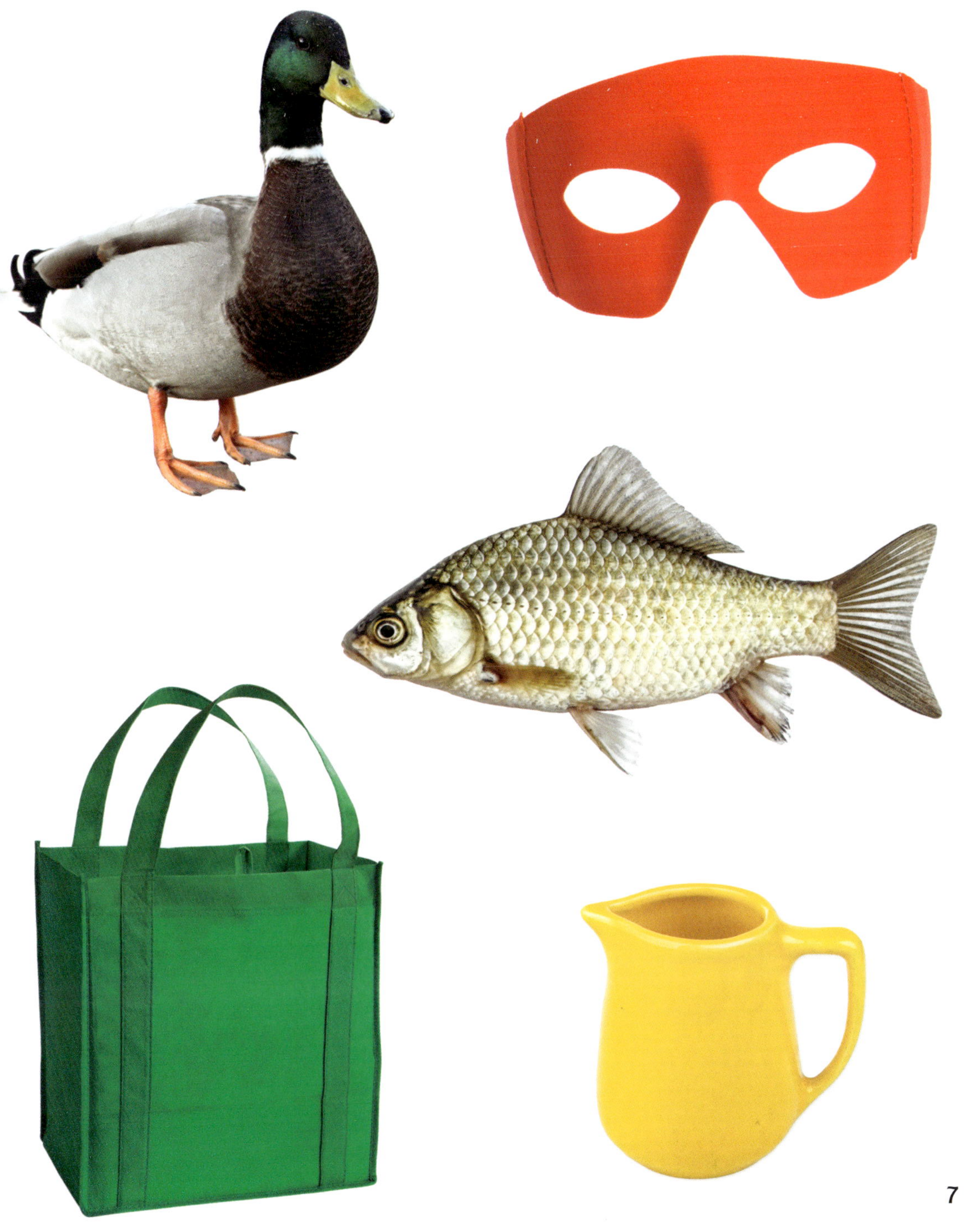

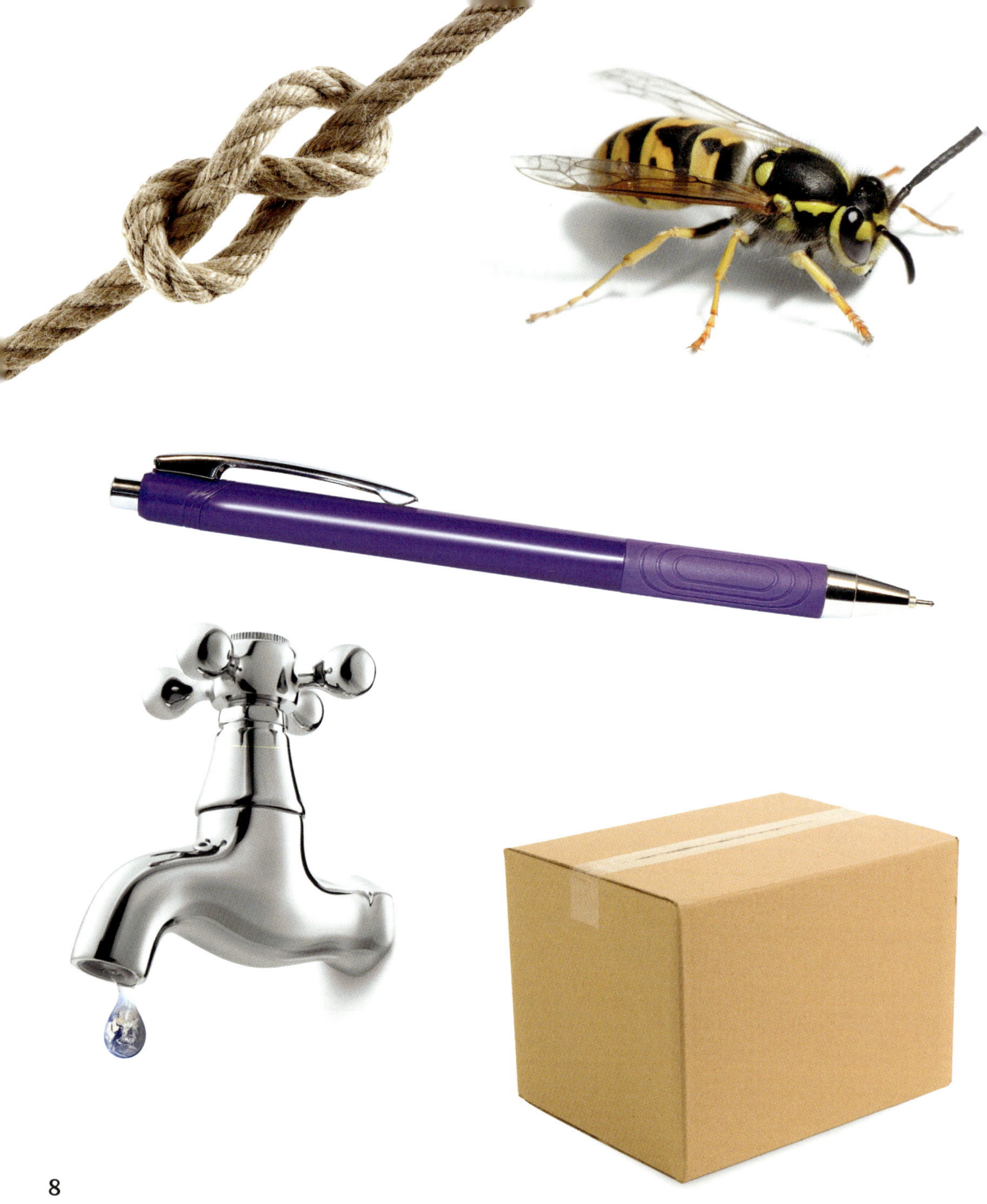